M000168930

Preface

The art of surfing was born along the shore waters of Hawai'i, the most remote
destination on the planet. To the native people of this place, **na kanaka maoli**,
this favorite pastime known as **he'e nalu** was more than just a sport.

The root word **he'e**, refers to the sliding, gliding movement and motion across the **nalu**,
the churning ocean or waves. But **nalu** has a deeper, more primal meaning that is com-
mon and essential to all human life, for **nalu** also refers to the fluid from which each
human being emerges to join the family of **kanaka** ~ man.

Like a new born child emerging from the depths of his mother's womb, a surfer is reborn
each time he struggles to the surface of the churning sea. As he rises from the depths
his lungs are filled with **Hā** ~ the breath of life, his face warmed by **ka Lā** ~ the sun,
and his skin caressed by **he makani 'olu'olu** ~ cool breezes.

Like those who **hula** on land, surfers dance both above and below the sea.
For some, it is like returning to the womb of **Papa** ~ Earth Mother.
For others it is the opportunity to reconnect, to reintegrate, to become **Pono** ~
to achieve inner peace, balance, harmony and calm, and to unify mind, body and spirit.

May the few moments spent immersed in this book remind you
of your connections to place, family and above all **mana** ~
the spirit and life energy that connects all things, one to the other.

E Mālama Pono!
(Take care, be well, stay integrated)

The things we love to do

Define us

Inspire us

Remind us who we are

In play we re-create

Live life out

Breathe life in

We pray in our own way

Our bodies become instruments

Improvising the sweet songs of our souls

This is the song of the Surfer Spirit...

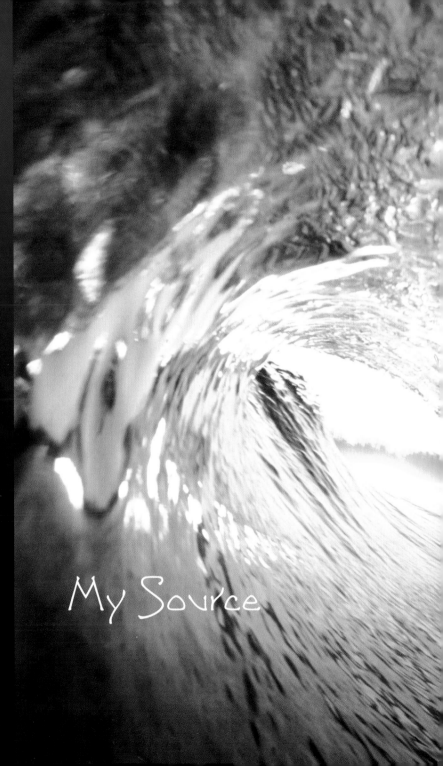

I must surf

Every day

I need to

Return to my element

My Source

I leave my troubles onshore as I dive into Bliss

I am free

I choose my challenges

I accept the outcomes

My wave

My ride

My life

My Choice

I remember that there are

beings in the world whom I must

Respect

Some days bring special gifts

I am honored

knowing that I am not alone

I Rejoice

No matter where I go in the world

I find others who share my Passion

I VALUE what is free

My "health club" is priceless

I know that life has its own rhythms

I Dance to Nature's Heartbeat

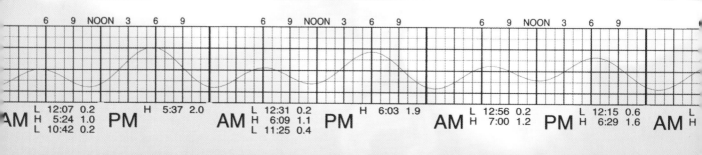

| | 6 | 9 | NOON | 3 | 6 | 9 | | | 6 | 9 | NOON | 3 | 6 | 9 | | | 6 | 9 | NOON | 3 | 6 | 9 | |

AM
L 12:07 0.2
H 5:24 1.0
L 10:42 0.2

PM
H 5:37 2.0

AM
L 12:31 0.2
H 6:09 1.1
L 11:25 0.4

PM
H 6:03 1.9

AM
L 12:56 0.2
H 7:00 1.2

PM
L 12:15 0.6
H 6:29 1.6

AM
L
H

6	9		6	9 NOON	3	6	9		6	9 NOON 3 6

L 1:23 0.8
H 6:56 1.4
AM

L 1:49 0.2
H 9:03 1.5
PM

L 3:03 0.9
H 7:26 1.1
AM

L 2:24 0.1
H 10:14 1.7
PM

L 5:32 0.8
H 8:08 0.9
AM

L 3:10 0.1
H 11:23 1.9
PM

L 7:
H 9:

Days of eternal calm remind me to reflect

I practice the virtue of Patience

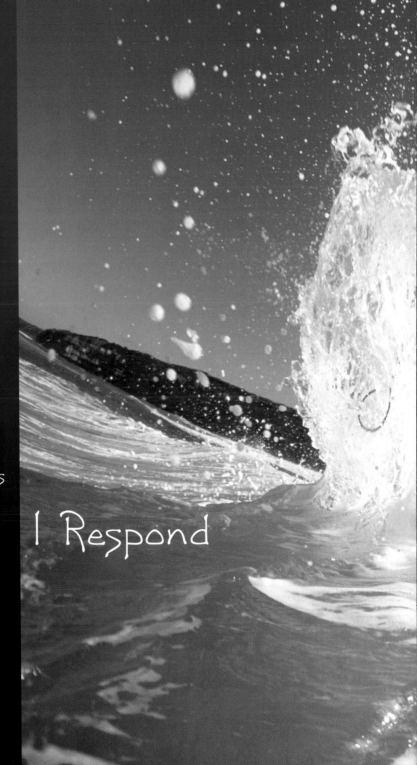

I am always prepared

When opportunity calls

I Respond

On less than epic days

I go out anyway and

I make the best of things

I know how to PLA

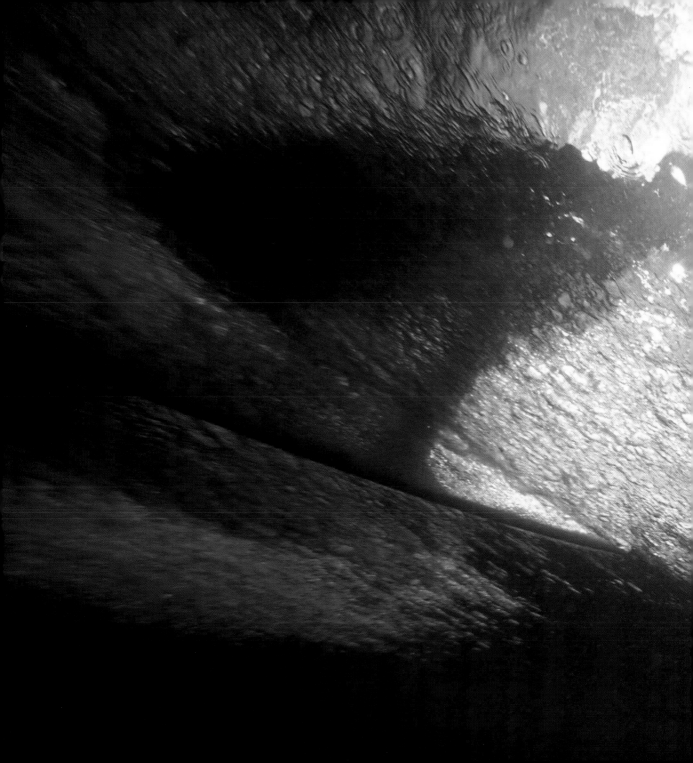

I know the best things in life

often require a risk

and learning   to fall well is part of life

I go with the flow and Surrender to life

I accept that sometimes you just have to eat it

I rise to life's challenges

I know the true meaning of COMMITMENT

I have faith

I know there will always be others greater than me

And those who

will follow my lead

I remain humble

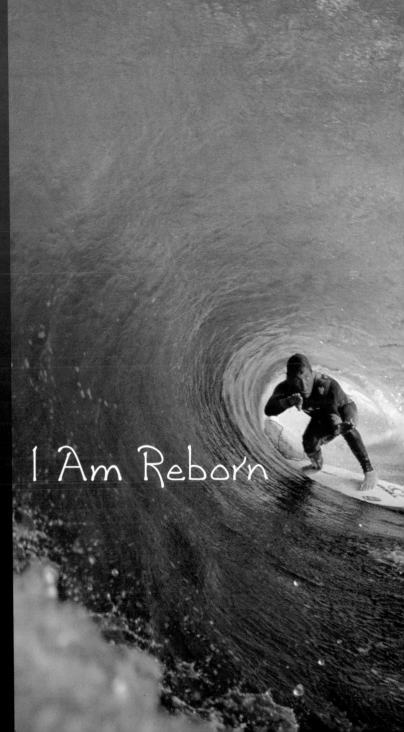

I go where

My spirit thrives

Soaring on water

Surging on adrenalin

I Am Reborn

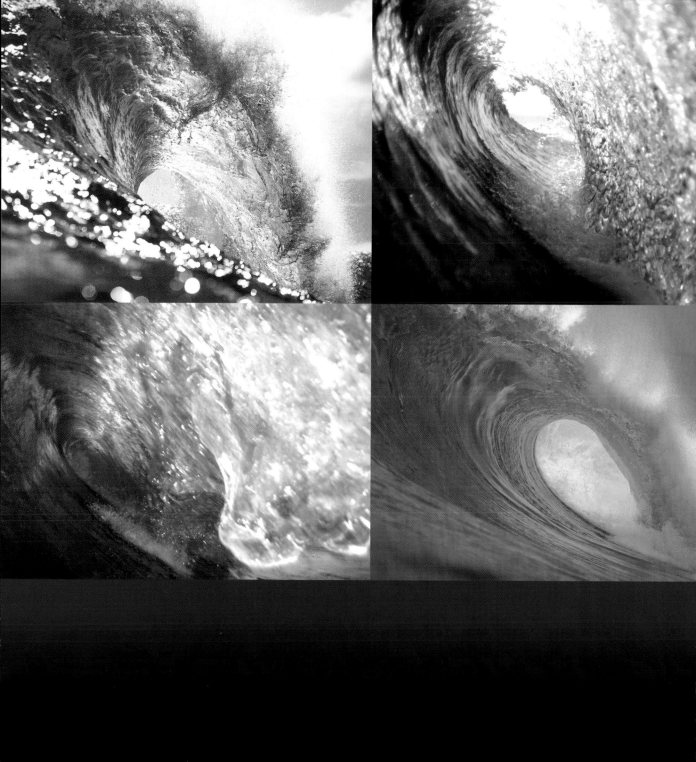

Time and time again

I Celebrate Life

I am a surfer

It's what I do

It's what I am

It is My Spirit

Surfing

Defines us

Inspires us

Reminds us who we are

We who surf

Live life out

Breathe life in

And pray in our own way

Our boards and bodies are

Instruments improvising

The sweet songs of our souls

Photos by John Bilderback

"Dawn Patrol"
Kaena Point from Sunset Beach,
O'ahu, Hawai'i.

"France Inside Out Barrel"
Dawn. Les Landes, France.

"Girl Duck Diving"
A hidden moment of grace.
Ehukai Beach Park, O'ahu, Hawai'i.

"Dawn Patrol 2"
Kaena Point from Sunset Beach,
O'ahu, Hawai'i.

"Dolphin"
Role models. Western Australia.

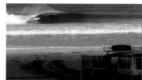

"JB's Love Shot"
Rushing too much to shut the
doors. Western Australia.

"Crystal Pipe Redux"
Mysteriously abducted by aliens
the whereabouts of the original
shot will torment me long into the
future.

"Above and Below"
The dance floor. Backdoor
Pipeline, O'ahu, Hawai'i.

"Taj Burrow Air"
Bird Rock, Victoria, Australia.

"Girl Power"
Serena Brooke and Rochelle
Ballard. Ehukai Beach Park,
O'ahu, Hawai'i.

"The Interface"
Lombok, Indonesia.

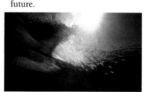

"Tamayo Pipe Drop"
Tamayo Perry. Pipeline, O'ahu,
Hawai'i.

"Lip Launch"
Perry Dane. Backdoor Pipeline
O'ahu, Hawai'i.

"The Rinse Cycle"
Inside the washing machine.
Pupukea, O'ahu, Hawai'i.

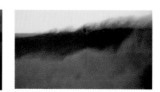

"Faith Sunset"
Pipeline, O'ahu, Hawai'i.

"Pipe Drop 11"
Chava Greenlee. Pipeline, O'ahu,
Hawai'i.

*'Future Sumbawan
World Surfing Champ"*
Lakey Pipe, Indonesia.

"Bold Enough"
Keoni Watson & Kelly Slater.
Hawai'i.

"Roar"
Kelly Slater, the surfer's surfer.
Waimea Bay, O'ahu, Hawai'i.

"Locked In"
Adam Replogle. Western Australia.

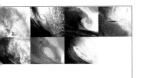

"Wave Series" (Partial)
Barrels from Tahiti, Australia,
Hawaii and Indonesia.

"Drop"
Unidentified Surfer in Hawai'i.

"Off the Lip"
Greg Pobst. Beach Haven,
New Jersey.

"Pipe Lip"
Pipeline, O'ahu, Hawai'i.

Photos by Jeff Devine

"Iceberg"~ Iceland, October 2003
Hawaiian surfers Ross Williams and Mikala Jones joined
Californian Jon Rose on a surf safari to Iceland. This ice floe
was on the west coast adjacent to the ocean. At the outflow was
a volcanic black sand beach where a small wave was peeling off
just outside. The surfers paddled out to the break through 30° F
water and around feeding sea lions that charged at them.

"Rainbow" ~ Pipeline, North Shore of O'ahu, Hawai'i.
This was taken straight in front of the break where surfers
gather to paddle out. A rainbow floated above the berm
but disapperared within minutes as the hard rains and
clouds moved in.

The Surfer Spirit Hui

Tim Anderson (Brother Timothy) ~ Copy Editor & Co-Writer

Tim is a poet, minister, traveler and creative consultant. He practices Ho'oponopono and draws his energy from all things natural. In addition to the "Spirit Series", his ongoing projects include collections of poems, psalms, short stories and screenwriting.

John Bilderback ~ Senior Staff Photographer, SURFER magazine

John blends two passions, surfing and photography, into an enviable career. He has been a staff photographer with SURFER Magazine for almost 20 years, traveling to surfing destinations such as Australia, Indonesia, Fiji, Tahiti, Peru, El Salvador, Mexico, and the Caribbean, as well as South Africa and Europe. Recently, John was awarded Kiteboarder Magazine's 2004 Photographer of the Year. He lives on O'ahu's North Shore with his wife Alexis. You can see more of his work at www.surfphotos.com and www.studiotwo.us

Jeff Devine ~ Photo Editor, Surfer's Journal · Staff Photographer and former Photo Editor, SURFER magazine

Jeff Devine has been shooting surfing, water sports and ocean scenes for 40 years. His work has been published worldwide. Jeff gained international attention documenting the first surfing trips to Iceland and Oman. His collective body of work from 1970-2005 constitutes the largest archive of historical surfing imagery in the world. Jeff currently travels on world pro surf safaris, and spends a month every year shooting the famous breaks on the North Shore of O'ahu, Hawai'i.

Ramsay Taum ~ Hawaiian Cultural Advisor & Kumu

Ramsay Taum is a Kumu (teacher) of several Native Hawaiian practices including Ho'oponopono (stress and conflict resolution), Lomi Haha (body alignment) and Kaihewalu lua (Hawaiian martial art). He is Director of Operations for The Hawai'i Nature Center, and Associate Director of the Native Hawaiian Hospitality Association where he consults on integrating Native Hawaiian cultural values and principals into contemporary business models. He serves on numerous boards, planning committees and advisory councils.

Special Thanks to:

Jim Elder (HaleKi'i) for his brilliant digital scanning and artistry.

Angela Lovitt, Esq. for her unending enthusiasm, advice and absolute support.

John & Diane Lovitt, for their kind guidance and generous hearts.

And to all our friends and family for their belief in us.

Photo: Val Loh

Jody Kjeldsen & Cynthia Derosier ~ Producers

These 2 local hapa-girls became sisters in surf.
We dedicate this book to all surfers who share our spirit,
and all those who love us anyway!

Photo: Val Loh

Here's to the next ride . . .

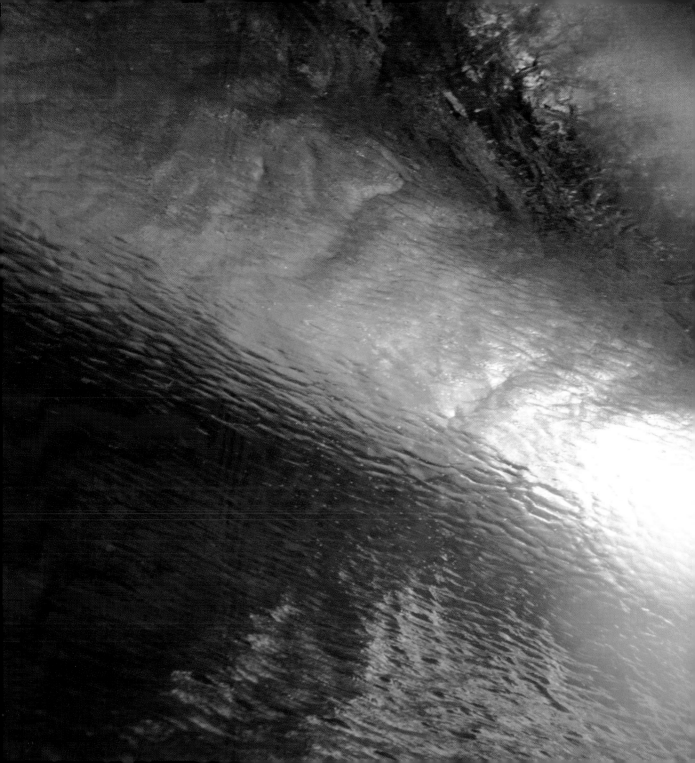

May this day bring you

A perfect ride on a perfect wave

A tale to tell

A memory for life ...

First Edition Printed: August 2005   •   Copyright © 2005 Free Time Productions, LLC
Published by Free Time Productions, LLC, P.O. Box 1677, Kailua, HI 96734
www.freetimepros.com

Library of Congress Cataloging-in Publication Data is available from Publisher.
Printed in Hong Kong.

To obtain additional copies of this book log onto
www. thespiritbooks.com

Printed with soy inks on 30% post-consumer recycled paper.

May your spirit continue to sing

E Mālama Pono